LEARNING ABOUT THE EARTH
Volcanoes

by Emily K. Green

BELLWETHER MEDIA • MINNEAPOLIS, MN

Note to Librarians, Teachers, and Parents:

Blastoff! Readers are carefully developed by literacy experts and combine standards-based content with developmentally appropriate text.

Level 1 provides the most support through repetition of high-frequency words, light text, predictable sentence patterns, and strong visual support.

Level 2 offers early readers a bit more challenge through varied simple sentences, increased text load, and less repetition of high-frequency words.

Level 3 advances early-fluent readers toward fluency through increased text and concept load, less reliance on visuals, longer sentences, and more literary language.

Whichever book is right for your reader, Blastoff! Readers are the perfect books to build confidence and encourage a love of reading that will last a lifetime!

This edition first published in 2007 by Bellwether Media.

No part of this publication may be reproduced in whole or in part without written permission of the publisher. For information regarding permission, write to Bellwether Media Inc., Attention: Permissions Department, Post Office Box 1C, Minnetonka, MN 55345-9998.

Library of Congress Cataloging-in-Publication Data
Green, Emily K., 1966–
    Volcanoes / by Emily K. Green.
        p. cm. — (Blastoff! readers) (Learning about the Earth)
Summary: "Simple text and supportive images introduce beginning readers to the physical characteristics of volcanoes."
    Includes bibliographical references and index.
    ISBN-10: 1-60014-041-6 (hardcover : alk. paper)
    ISBN-13: 978-1-60014-041-9 (hardcover : alk. paper)
    1. Volcanoes–Juvenile literature. I. Title. II. Series.

    QE521.3.G729 2007
    551.21–dc22   2006000607

Table of Contents

A volcano is a hole in the earth. A volcano is also the land around the hole.

Volcanoes have many shapes. Some volcanoes look like tall, steep mountains.

Some volcanoes look like big, low hills.

Some volcanoes rise up from the ocean floor. A volcano that rises above the surface of the water is called an island.

The hole in a volcano goes down deep inside the earth. Hot, melted rock called **magma** flows deep inside the earth.

Gas inside the earth can mix with the magma and build **pressure**. This pressure can push magma up toward the surface.

A volcano may rumble and smoke when pressure builds underneath it.

The pressure builds and builds. Finally, magma comes to the surface in an **eruption**.

Different volcanoes have different kinds of eruptions. This eruption is a big cloud of smoke and **ash**.

The wind blows the smoke and ash a long way. The ash falls back to the ground like snow.

A big eruption blasts the hole open even wider. The top of the hole is called the **crater**.

This eruption is a
fountain of fire.

Magma that comes out of a volcano is called **lava**. This lava explodes into the air.

This lava flows slowly on the ground. Lava can crush or burn everything in its path.

Some volcanoes are **extinct**.
Extinct volcanoes will not
erupt again.

Some volcanoes are **dormant**. A dormant volcano can lie quietly for a long time. Then suddenly it can erupt.

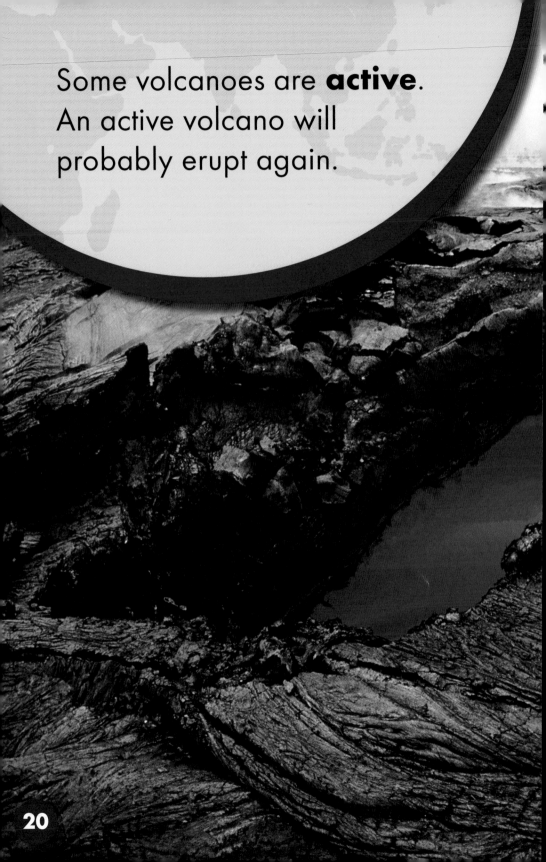

Some volcanoes are **active**.
An active volcano will
probably erupt again.

Scientists try to **predict** when a volcano will erupt. They want to warn people to get far out of the way.

Glossary

active—a volcano that has pressure from hot magma and gases underneath it

ash—tiny, burnt bits of rock

crater—the opening of the hole in a volcano; the crater of an extinct volcano may fill with water and become a lake.

dormant—a volcano that is quiet but may become active again

eruption—when hot magma rises to the surface of the earth in a volcano

extinct—dead; will not be active again

gas—invisible material that floats in the air; gas is mixed with melted rock deep inside the earth.

lava—magma that has come out of a volcano

magma—hot, melted rock inside the earth

predict—to say when something might happen in the future

pressure—force

scientists—people who study something

To Learn More

AT THE LIBRARY
Berger, Melvin and Gilda. *Why Do Volcanoes Blow Their Tops?: Questions and Answers About Volcanoes and Earthquakes*. New York: Scholastic, 2000.

Furgang, Kathy. *Mount St. Helens: The Smoking Mountain*. New York: PowerKids Press. 2001.

Nordenstrom, Michael. *Pele and the Rivers of Fire*. Honolulu, HI: Bess Press, 2002.

ON THE WEB
Learning more about volcanoes is as easy as 1, 2, 3.

1. Go to www.factsurfer.com

2. Enter "volcanoes" into search box.

3. Click the "Surf" button and you will see a list of related web sites.

With factsurfer.com, finding more information is just a click away.

Index

The photographs in this book are reproduced through the courtesy of: G Brad Lewis/Getty Images, front cover, pp. 16-17, 20-21; Oliver Strewe/Getty Images, pp. 4-5; John Pennock/Getty Images, p. 5; Bruce Heinemann/Getty Images, p. 6; David Wall/Getty Images, p. 7; Macduff Everton/Getty Images, p. 8; Jumpstart Studios/Getty Images, p. 9; Jerry Driendl/Getty Images, p. 10; Carsten Peter/Getty Images, pp. 10-11; Klaus Nigge/Getty Images, pp. 12-13; David Trood/Getty Images, pp. 14-15; Jim Sugar/Getty Images, p. 17; Bobby Haas/Getty Images, p. 18; Kirk Anderson/Getty Images, p. 19.